THE BATTLE FOR OIL

UNDERSTANDING GLOBAL ISSUES

Published by Weigl Publishers Inc.
350 5th Avenue, Suite 3304, PMB 6G
New York, NY 10118-0069
Website: www.weigl.com

This book is based on *The Battle for Oil: Diplomacy, Politics and Big Business*
Copyright ©2003 Understanding Global Issues Ltd., Cheltenham, England

Library of Congress Cataloging-in-Publication Data
Wells, Donald, editor.
The battle for oil / Donald Wells.
    p. cm. -- (Understanding global issues)
  Includes bibliographical references and index.
  ISBN 1-59036-235-7 (library binding : alk. paper) — ISBN 1-59036-509-7 (pbk.)
  1. Petroleum industry and trade--Political aspects. 2. Petroleum industry and trade--
Political aspects--Middle East. 3. Petroleum industry and trade--Political aspects--
United States. 4. United States--Foreign relations--Middle East. 5. Middle East--
Foreign relations--United States. 6. World politics--21st century. I. Title. II. Series.
  HD9560.6.W45 2005
  333.8'232--dc22

                        2004007074
             Printed in the United States of America
                1 2 3 4 5 6 7 8 9 0 10 09 08 07 06

EDITOR Donald Wells **DESIGNER** Terry Paulhus

Contents

Introduction

Petroleum, or oil as it is commonly known, is one of the foundations of modern civilization. Without it, industrial society would grind to a halt. Cars, trucks, aircraft, and ships depend on petroleum, as do numerous industries ranging from **pharmaceuticals** to plastics. Since oil is vital for modern life, it is not surprising that the oil industry is closely associated with politics and that governments regard the security of their oil supply as a key strategic issue.

Asia and the West's dependence on imported oil is growing. Some people have attributed U.S. foreign policy on Iraq as a battle for oil. There is no doubt, of course, that having the world's second largest oil reserves makes Iraq a valuable piece of real estate. Several companies are trying to buy oil rights in Iraq, including the French company TotalFinaElf, the Chinese National Petroleum Company, and Russia's Lukoil. Because France , China, and Russia are permanent members of the United Nations (UN) Security Council, and the United States and Great Britain are the main occupying countries in Iraq, some people believe that

▬▬ **One barrel of crude oil produces about 20 gallons (76 liters) of engine gasoline.**

the war in Iraq was fought to gain control of Iraq's oil reserves. Other people think competition for oil rights in Iraq is part of the continuing international struggle for oil resources that has always characterized the oil industry.

Petroleum is one of the foundations of modern civilization.

Some people have argued that the war in Afghanistan was an excuse to extend U.S. military presence to Central Asia, where Russia had previously controlled extensive, but undeveloped, oil and gas resources. Other people believe that this war will result in stronger trade ties between oil-producing and oil-consuming countries, which will contribute to peace and stability.

The Organization of Petroleum Exporting Countries' (OPEC) oil price hike in 1973 and 1974, the Iranian Revolution in 1979 to 1980, and the first Gulf War in 1990 to 1991 created serious disruptions in the oil supply and caused problems for the world's economy. There is little doubt that **industrialized** countries would want to protect their economies from shocks caused by upheavals in the oil industry.

Although oil is viewed as a cause of environmental degradation, it is still the most important form of energy in industrialized countries. However, the oil industry is not immune to social concerns. Its employees are just as worried as other citizens about climate change, pollution, injustice, and war. It has been said that the age of oil is coming to an end. This may be happening not just because oil reserves are running low, but because the social and environmental costs of oil are becoming too high to maintain.

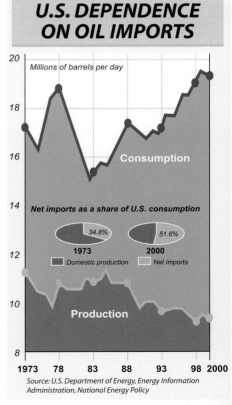

U.S. DEPENDENCE ON OIL IMPORTS

Millions of barrels per day

Consumption

Net imports as a share of U.S. consumption

34.8% 1973
51.6% 2000

■ Domestic production □ Net imports

Production

1973 78 83 88 93 98 2000

Source: U.S. Department of Energy, Energy Information Administration, National Energy Policy

A Hydrocarbon History

The development of the oil industry in the United States in the late nineteenth century coincided with the rapid growth of industry. Oil formed strong ties with the automobile industry and helped spawn the petrochemical and plastics industries.

The early oil wells in Pennsylvania, developed after Edwin Drake's discovery in 1859, produced oil wells suited for lamp lighting and machine lubrication. Just as electricity was making kerosene lamps obsolete, motor vehicles appeared on the scene, and their popularity spread across the United States. Unlike Europe, where urban areas were densely populated and public transportation was popular, the United States developed a car-based society, with cities sprawling over large areas. In the United States, cheap gasoline came to be regarded as an essential part of daily life, like water and electricity.

As the car culture developed in other countries, they also became dependent on cheap oil. Nowhere, however, is per capita oil consumption as high as in the United States, where there are more than 750 vehicles for every 1,000 people. The average vehicle is driven more than 12,000 miles

The United States consumes almost 9 million barrels of gasoline daily—about 43 percent of the daily global gasoline consumption.

(20,000 kilometers) a year, and the average price of a gallon of gasoline is less than half the typical price in Europe. Car dependency and a host of oil-based industries, such as chemicals, plastics, vehicles, and aerospace, make the United States especially dependent on oil.

John D. Rockefeller's company Standard Oil became a dominant force in the early history of the world's oil industry. Even after the anti-trust breakup of Standard Oil in 1911, its successor companies remained the largest players in the world oil market. On the global scene, the main rivals of these

companies were Royal Dutch/Shell, founded in 1902, and British Petroleum, which grew out of the Anglo-Persian Oil Company founded

---

Oil has played a key role in modern wars.

---

in 1909. In short, a handful of giant oil companies in **developed countries** controlled global supplies and made vast profits from the oil they pumped in **developing countries**. After 1945, a post-colonial atmosphere prevailed, and producer countries began to take control of their oil reserves. For example, some producer countries nationalized their oil assets, and others formed OPEC, which quadrupled oil prices in the early 1970s. The OPEC price increases led the United States to introduce fuel economy measures for auto makers in the 1970s to reduce its dependency on imported oil. In spite of these measures, light vehicles, which include cars, light trucks, and

sport utility vehicles (SUVs), only average 20 miles per gallon (8.5 km/L). In 2003, U.S. oil imports reached 9.6 million barrels (1.5 million cubic meters) a day.

Oil has played a key role in modern wars. In the early twentieth century, the decision to use oil instead of coal to power ships made fleets faster and less expensive to operate. The United States' plentiful supply of oil was crucial to the Allied victory in both World Wars. The British destruction of the Romanian oil fields in late 1916 prevented the Germans from acquiring a key resource.

In World War II, Hitler's invasion of Russia was partly aimed at controlling the **Caucasus** oil fields. Japan's attack on Pearl Harbor was partly a response to the 1940 U.S. oil embargo, aimed at curbing Japanese imperialism. Oil is not only essential for transportation and industry, it is also a vital component of military power.

MAJOR COMPANIES IN THE OIL INDUSTRY

John D. Rockefeller was the first oil baron, and his company, Standard Oil, became the most powerful company in the United States. Its hold on energy resources became a serious political issue, and in 1911, Standard Oil was split into smaller units. Some of the descendants of Standard Oil—ExxonMobil, Chevron, Conoco, Amoco, and Arco—are still major players in the global oil industry. The industry itself, however, is more competitive than ever, with numerous large companies, many of them state owned, competing for oil supplies around the world.

ORGANIZATION OF PETROLEUM EXPORTING COUNTRIES (OPEC)

The Organization of Petroleum Exporting Countries (OPEC) was formed in 1960 at a conference in Baghdad, Iraq. Its aim was to coordinate members' petroleum policies and safeguard their interests. The five original members—Iran, Iraq, Kuwait, Saudi Arabia, and Venezuela—were soon joined by Algeria, Indonesia, Libya, Nigeria, Qatar, and the United Arab Emirates (UAE). Ecuador and Gabon were members for some years, but both countries dropped out in the 1990s.

The 11 OPEC countries produce about 40 percent of the world's oil and hold about 78 percent of the world's proved oil reserves. OPEC influence was at its height in the early 1970s when as part of Arab efforts to force Israel to comply with UN resolutions on the Palestinian issue it proposed an embargo on supplies to the West and quadrupled the price of oil. This was the first time the "oil weapon" had been used by producer countries to influence international politics. OPEC is more cautious these days. Its power had diminished by the end of the Cold War, when the Former Soviet Union (FSU) and other producer countries joined the market but chose not to join OPEC.

In early 2003, despite an OPEC target of $22 to $28 a barrel, which was well above a free market price, the Iraq "war premium" and the Venezuelan strike had pushed New York-traded crude oil to $38 a barrel. High oil prices suit non-OPEC producers such as Mexico and Russia, but they penalize importers such as Europe, Japan, and the United States.

Some experts argue that OPEC's destruction is part of U.S. foreign policy. The theory is that a post-Saddam Hussein Iraq would leave OPEC, increase oil production, and cause prices to fall, which would benefit the industrialized world. Others point out that Iraq's oil **infrastructure** is in desperate need of upgrading, and it will take many years before Iraq's oil will affect the global oil market.

KEY CONCEPTS

Edwin Drake On August 28, 1859, former railroad conductor Edwin Drake struck oil. Using **cable-tool drilling** techniques for salt wells, he drilled 69 feet (21 m) into a patch of land in Titusville, Pennsylvania. He produced a steady flow of 25 barrels of oil per day. Drake marketed the oil for heating and lighting.

Proved recoverable reserves means the amount of fossil fuel resource that is reasonably certain to be commercially recoverable using current technology. One of the oddities of the fossil fuel industry is that these reserves are larger now than they were 20 years ago. This is the result of new discoveries and better recovery technology. Company estimates of proved reserves are subject to independent audit and tend to err on the conservative side. Proved reserves are much lower than resources that are eventually recovered or total oil in the ground.

Born: July 8, 1839, near Richford, New York

Died: May 23, 1937, in Ormond Beach, Florida

Legacy: Established several philanthropic organizations, including The Rockefeller Foundation, which has given assistance to groups concerned with public health, medical education, increasing food production, scientific advancement, social research, and the arts.

Navigate to **voteview.uh.edu/ entrejdr.htm** for information about John D. Rockefeller.

People in Focus

John Davison Rockefeller was the guiding force behind the creation and development of the Standard Oil Company. Rockefeller was also one of the first major **philanthropists** in the United States, establishing several important foundations and donating a total of $540 million to charity.

Rockefeller was spectacular in business because he was hard working, very competitive, and a skilled business strategist and forecaster. He embodied a rare combination of caution, precision with imagination, and resolve.

In 1859, Rockefeller became a partner in a produce business, and 4 years later, with his partners Samuel Andrews, Maurice Clark, and Clark's brothers, he established an oil refinery.

In 1870, he and his associates—including S. V. Harkness, H. M. Flagler, and his brother William—organized the Standard Oil Company of Ohio. By enforcing strict economy and efficiency, through mergers and agreements with competitors, and by ruthlessly crushing weaker competitors, Rockefeller soon dominated the U.S. oil-refining industry. As a result of its near monopoly of the oil business in the United States, Standard Oil Company was forced to split into smaller companies in 1911.

Rockefeller retired at the age of 58 and devoted the rest of his life to being a philanthropist. Rockefeller was worth $900 million in 1913. As a result of his philanthropy and the trusts he set up for his heirs, his net worth was less than $25 million when he died.

Dependence on Oil

O il is the lifeblood of modern society. It accounts for 40 percent of primary energy use and 95 percent of vehicle fuel. Total world oil demand in 2003 was 77 million barrels (12 million m^3) a day. As world economic growth continues, crude oil demand is expected to rise to 100 million barrels (16 million m^3) day by 2015, with U.S. demand forecast to be about 26 million barrels (4 million m^3) a day.

In autumn 2000, public protests over fuel taxes in Great Britain led to weeks of uncertainty and panic buying. It was a reminder that modern civilization depends on a regular supply of oil. Securing that supply is a key strategic goal of governments everywhere.

The United States was self-sufficient in oil until the 1950s. Net imports overtook domestic production for the first time in 1998. In 2004, oil imports accounted for 58 percent of U.S. oil consumption. The United States Department of Energy's *Annual Energy Outlook 2004* report predicts that U.S. dependence on oil imports will rise to 70 percent by 2025. The National Energy Policy Development Group, headed by U.S. Vice-President Dick Cheney, urged President George W. Bush to make energy security a priority of trade and foreign policy.

■■■ **In his 2006 State of the Union address, U.S. President George W. Bush coined the phrase "America is addicted to oil," echoing a position stated by former President Jimmy Carter nearly 30 years earlier.**

Domestic crude oil production in the United States peaked in 1970 and has fallen steadily since , except for a brief surge caused by the development of the oil industry in Alaska in the 1980s. The United States obtains more than 40 percent of its imported oil from Canada, Mexico, and Venezuela, 20 percent from Persian Gulf countries, and 14 percent from Africa. In 2003, Canada supplied 16 percent of the oil imported by the United States. Saudi Arabia supplied 15 percent. Mexico supplied 13 percent, and Venezuela supplied 10 percent. A strike in Venezuela stopped that country's oil production in 2002 and 2003, which emphasized the need for the United States to have a wide variety of sources for imported oil.

The European Union (EU) also depends heavily on imported oil, which accounts for more than 65 percent of its oil consumption. Much of this oil comes from the Middle East and Africa. Japan, the world's second-largest oil importer, has almost no oil resources. It imports 99 percent of its oil and buys 80 percent of this oil from the Middle East. Convoys of tankers carry more than 4 million barrels (640,000 m^3) a day from the Persian Gulf to Japan.

Until the 1980s, the bulk of the global demand for oil came from industrialized countries. The Organization for Economic Cooperation and Development (OECD), with 18 percent of

"Very large capacity carriers," or VLCCs, can carry more than 1.6 million barrels (250,000 m^3) of crude oil.

the world's population, accounts for 62 percent of global oil consumption, or 48 million barrels (7.6 million m^3) a day. The United States alone accounts for 25 percent of global oil consumption. However, the developing world is also

---

Japan imports 99 percent of its oil.

---

beginning to use more oil. Asia already uses six times more oil than its resources can provide.

China's growing need for oil imports has become an

important new factor in world oil. China's daily use of oil is expected to reach 10.5 million barrels (1.7 million m^3) a day by 2020—more than double its 2000 level. Car sales are booming in China, and Japanese car manufacturers are busy building massive factories to meet this new demand. Although car density in China is still very low, it is increasing at more than one million cars a year, which means a growing need for oil.

China is developing new oil resources offshore and in the Xinjiang Uygur Autonomous Region and Tibet, but it has to import about 75 percent of its oil supply.

The Chinese National Petroleum Company (CNPC) has negotiated **concessions** in Azerbaijan, Iran, Kazakhstan, Iraq, Peru, Venezuela, and Sudan. There have also been discussions about long-distance pipelines being built to carry oil and gas from Central Asia to China. However, these projects have been delayed by doubts about political stability, the size of Central Asia's oil and gas reserves, and costs involved in building these pipelines.

Proposed Central Asian projects include a pipeline from Irkutsk to Beijing, backed by Russia's Yukos Oil; and a pipeline to take Russian crude oil from Siberia to the Pacific Coast port of Nakhodka proposed by Russian operator Transneft. This would enable Russian oil to be exported to China, Japan, Korea, and other markets.

CNPC has negotiated important oil deals in Iraq,

As more countries become even more dependent on oil, the battle for resources will increase.

---

and it is keen to see the situation in that country stabilized. Meanwhile, CNPC has a stake in the Greater Nile Petroleum Operating Company, and it is developing oil fields in southern Sudan, which began oil exports in 1999. Oil has complicated the long civil war that has raged in Sudan in recent decades between its Muslim-Arab rulers, based in Khartoum, and African rebel groups in the south. Tribes living in the oil regions have had their lives severely disrupted.

Korea, both the poverty-stricken communist North and the prosperous, free market South, depends heavily on oil imports. In 1994, the United States agreed to supply North Korea with 551,156 tons (500,000 t) of heavy oil a year as part of a deal to stop North Korea from pursuing a nuclear

KEY CONCEPTS

Crude oil is 82 to 87 percent carbon. Most of the balance is hydrogen, although sulphur and trace heavy metals may also be present. Crude oil varies greatly from place to place, depending on the particular process that created it. The light oils of Pennsylvania and the Persian Gulf are particularity suitable for vehicle fuel. Crude oil has to be refined before it can be used. Typically, it is pumped to a refinery where aviation fuel, gasoline, and diesel fuel are drawn off at different stages of the process.

Oil fields are graded according to size. There are megagiants, which have more than 50 billion barrels (8 billion m^3)of oil; supergiants, which have 5 billion to 50 billion barrels (790 million to 8 billion m^3) of oil; giants, which have 500 million to 5 billion barrels (80 to 790 million m^3) of oil; majors, which have 100 to 500 million barrels (16 to 80 million m^3) of oil; down to tiny oil fields. So far, two megagiants have been discovered—al-Ghawar in Saudi Arabia, which has 86 billion barrels (14 billion m^3) of oil, and al-Burqan in Kuwait, which has 75 billion barrels (12 billion m^3) of oil. About 40 supergiants, 300 giants, and 1,000 majors have been discovered.

Organization for Economic Cooperation and Development (OECD) is a group of 30 countries that discuss, develop, and refine economic and social policies. They compare experiences, seek answers to common problems, and work to coordinate domestic and international policies to help members and nonmembers deal with an increasingly globalized world. Member countries are committed to pluralistic democracy and a market economy. The members include Australia, Austria, Belgium, Canada, Czech Republic, Denmark, Finland, France, Germany, Great Britain, Greece, Hungary, Iceland, Ireland, Italy, Japan, Korea, Luxembourg, Mexico, Netherlands, New Zealand, Norway, Poland, Portugal, Slovak Republic, Spain, Sweden, Switzerland, Turkey, and the United States.

energy program that could produce weapons-grade plutonium. The Bush administration hardened the U.S. position in December 2002 by cutting off the oil supply after North Korea announced it had resumed its nuclear weapons program.

Almost every country has an economy that depends on oil. For producer countries, oil provides a vital source of export revenue. For consumer countries, oil provides the means to run transportation systems, generate electricity, lubricate factory machines, and operate petrochemical industries that produce plastics, fertilizers, textiles, and cosmetics. As more countries become even more dependent on oil, it is possible the battle for oil resources will increase.

After the September 11, 2001, terrorist attacks on New York and Washington, D.C., EU ministers decided to pay more attention to the security of the EU's oil supply. As a result, they have proposed new rules for stockpiling oil supplies. All member states except Great Britain, which is a producer country with oil in the ground, have been asked to build a strategic oil reserve that would last 120 days. This is even longer than the 90 days' supply recommended by the OECD's International Energy Agency. Japan and South Korea, both heavily dependent on oil imports, require refinery operators to maintain minimum stock levels to cope with fluctuations in supply. In 2003, China and India decided to create strategic oil reserves in order to avoid the effects of disruptions to the oil supply. The United States keeps about 600 million barrels (9.5 million m^3) of oil in its Strategic Petroleum Reserve, which was established in the mid-1970s.

During the 1991 Gulf War, Iraqi troops dumped 8 million barrels of oil into the Persian Gulf and set fire to more than 600 oil wells.

Global Oil Resources

The geological formations that create hydrocarbon, or oil, deposits are found from the Arctic to the continental shelves of West Africa and East Asia. Many remote areas are not yet fully explored, which means that more large fields may be found. However, most oil comes from giant fields that have been producing for many years. Of the 120 or so fields that are producing more than 100,000 barrels (16,000 m^3) a day, half were discovered in the 1960s or before. Although thousands of oil fields have been discovered since then, the discovery of new giant oil fields has been rare. The discovery of the last oil field able to produce one million barrels (160,000 m^3) a day occurred in Mexico's Cantarell oil field in 1976. Only three other discoveries in the past 20 years produce more than 200,000 barrels (32,000 m^3) a day— Marlim in Brazil, Cusiama in Colombia, and Draugen in Norway.

Some argue that world oil production is close to its peak and will soon begin to decline. The experience of the United States is often quoted as an indication of what is likely to happen on a global scale. M. K. Hubbert's theory that U.S. oil output would peak around 1970, when half its total resource had

---

Most oil comes from giant oil fields that have been producing for many years.

---

been pumped, proved accurate. Some experts argue that human beings have already burned about 950 billion barrels (150 billion m^3) of oil, almost half the planet's estimated recoverable reserves. It is obvious that an oil field cannot be pumped forever, but so far, predictions that the world's oil would soon run out have not been accurate.

In its *World Petroleum Assessment 2000*, the U.S. Geological Survey estimated the total of "undiscovered conventional oil resources and reserve growth" at about 3 trillion barrels (500 billion m^3). This is much higher than most other estimates—typically around 2 trillion barrels (300 billion m^3)—and about three times the total of proved reserves shown by British Petroleum (BP) in its statistical review for 2002. The BP figure is assumed to be conservative because it only counts known fields that "geological and engineering information indicates with reasonable certainty can be recovered in the future from known **reservoirs** under existing economic and operating conditions." Reserves of shale oil and oil sands are not included. These forms of oil are often too costly to harvest, partly for environmental reasons.

■ **Four areas account for 78 percent of U.S. crude oil reserves: Texas (25%), Alaska (24%), California (17%), and the Gulf of Mexico (13%).**

PROVED OIL RESERVES
(thousand million barrels at the end of 2005)

Saudi Arabia	264.2	Libya	39.1
Iraq	115.0	China	16.0
Iran	137.5	United States	29.3
Kuwait	101.5	Qatar	19.6
United Arab Emirates	97.8	Mexico	13.7
Russia	74.4	Algeria	12.2
Venezuela	79.7	Norway	9.7
Nigeria	35.9		

Source: BP Statistical Review of World Energy June 2006

Hundreds of new oil fields have come online in recent years. Major discoveries have been made in Angola, Ecuador, Equatorial Guinea, and Vietnam. However, no oil fields comparable in size to the giants of the Persian Gulf area have been discovered for many years. The world's largest oil field is al-Ghawar in Saudi Arabia. This oil field covers 888 square miles (2,300 sq km) and still contains 70 billion barrels (11 billion m^3) of oil, more than twice the total oil reserves of the entire United States. Saudi Arabia also has the world's largest offshore oil field at Safaniya. Kashagan in Kazakh Caspian, which has 10 to 20 billion barrels (1.6 to 3.2 billion m^3) of oil; Iran's Azadegan, which has 30 to 40 billion barrels (4.8 to 6.4 billion m^3) of oil; and Iraq's western desert, which has 100 billion barrels of oil, are three giant oil fields that are still undeveloped. These oil fields are the subject of hard bargaining between governments and oil companies.

Elsewhere, oil has been found in tropical forest areas, coastal waters, and the Arctic. Extracting oil from such places requires large fields and a high oil price to make the project worthwhile. Meanwhile, the life of existing oil fields has been prolonged by improvements in technology, which make oil extraction possible from previously unreachable areas.

The discovery of oil and gas in the North Sea in 1969 was a

The world's largest oil field is al-Ghawar in Saudi Arabia.

---

stroke of luck for Great Britain. This discovery transformed Great Britain's energy resources and its finances. However, the most accessible oil fields have already been tapped, and North Sea production, after peaking in 1999, is slowly declining. Subsea oil is expensive to produce and is, therefore, vulnerable to changes in global oil prices. An oil price below $20 a barrel would make North Sea oil too expensive to extract. Saudi Arabia, by contrast, could still make a profit if the price of oil was $2 a barrel.

Siberian oil is relatively expensive because it has to be extracted from **permafrost** areas and then transported long distances over land. During the Soviet era, the vast resources of Central Asia and Siberia were poorly developed. The opening up of the Former Soviet Union's (FSU) oil and gas reserves has been the most exciting event in the oil industry in recent decades. As western companies sought to get a foothold in the region, many deals were attempted, half-agreed, and then abandoned. Only a few deals went ahead. One major problem was determining who in the FSU had the authority to make these deals. Another was the tenacity of Russian negotiators determined to keep control of resources and pipelines.

Since the breakup of the Soviet Union, Russian oil and gas companies have become major players in global energy, with massive reserves and major concessions in Iran, Iraq, and other countries. The FSU is estimated to have 40 percent of the world's long-term gas reserves and 5 percent of its oil.

The North Sea experience proved invaluable in the development of offshore oil technology. Subsea oil production, sometimes in water 1.2 miles (2 km) deep, is one of the most remarkable

KEY CONCEPTS

Geological formations The geological formations that create oil and gas deposits contain unique ingredients. These include source rocks full of organic material; porous reservoirs for oil or gas to accumulate; sufficient heat and time to "cook" the sediments; impermeable cap rocks; and traps, or areas in the ground that stop the flow of oil and gas. Each of these ingredients has to be present and occur in the correct order and at the right time in order for gas and oil to form.

■ **Deep drilling in the Gulf of Mexico accounts for nearly half of all U.S. offshore oil production.**

achievements in engineering. Some people wonder why similar efforts cannot be made to find a substitute for oil. In fact, scientists have been trying to do just that for years, but oil has many advantages that are hard to beat. In addition, the infrastructure developed after a century of oil use will be very expensive to change. For these reasons, there is great reluctance to abandon the use of oil.

WORLD ENERGY CONSUMPTION BY FUEL TYPE, 1980 TO 2020

Despite environmental concerns, projections suggest that oil will remain the top global energy source for many decades. The graph shows the U.S. Energy Information Administration's (EIA) estimate of past and future energy consumption, converted into **British thermal units** (Btu). Note the growing importance of natural gas and the slow growth in the use of renewable sources of energy.

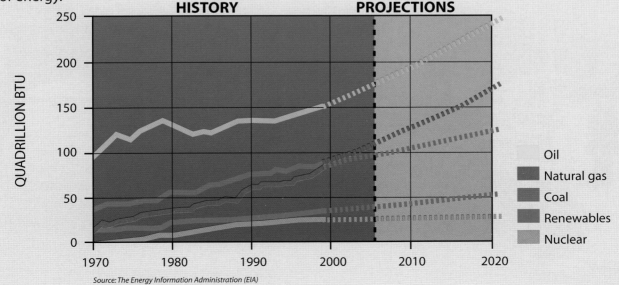

Source: The Energy Information Administration (EIA)

Controlling the Supply of Oil

While U.S. oil companies have always been privately owned, other countries preferred to keep some or all of their oil and gas industry under government control—at least until the wave of **privatization** took hold in the 1990s. The threat of nationalization, which deprived western oil companies of their assets in Iran, Iraq, Kuwait, Libya, and Nigeria in the 1970s, has largely disappeared. At the same time, the oil business has become more competitive as new entrants have joined the market, including some state-owned enterprises that have learned to pursue aggressive overseas expansion.

In the 1970s, OPEC countries supplied as much as 90 percent of global oil exports.

> *In the post-colonial era, it has not been possible to control foreign oil supplies directly.*

This virtual monopoly gave them the chance to set their own price on the world market. Their decision to quadruple the price in 1973 caused economic chaos around the world and set in motion a global flood of petrodollars. This sudden wealth was accompanied by a surge in armament sales and the growth of offshore financial centers keen to handle Arab money.

OPEC's use of the oil weapon also changed the world in other ways. Security of the oil supply became a primary concern of western governments. The United States poured weapons into Egypt, Iran, Iraq, Israel, Saudi Arabia, and Turkey as it sought to win friends in the

■ In the 1970s, Middle Eastern oil shipments were halted, causing a major energy crisis in many industrialized countries.

oil-rich Middle East. With its own oil production falling, the oil fields of the Persian Gulf area took on a new importance.

In the post-colonial era, it has not been possible to control foreign oil supplies directly. Therefore, it has been necessary to use other forms of influence. This has led to some unusual relationships as regimes have come in and out of favor. Thus, Iran, a key U.S. ally under the Shah, became a **pariah** state under Ayatollah Khomeini. Iraq, a major recipient of U.S. military aid in the 1980s, later became the focus of President George W. Bush's "axis of evil." Regime change in Iraq became the rallying cry for U.S. policy in the Middle East, which caused other countries in the region to become concerned. Would a

war to remove Saddam Hussein from power in Iraq bring more stability to the oil market and increase the supplies of oil? Would it generate instability and make oil more expensive and slow down global economic recovery? The risks were great.

Saddam Hussein's transformation from western ally to villain has had a serious effect on Middle East oil production. Bringing Iraq back into the free market is important because there is the potential for instability in Saudi Arabia, and the continuing deadlock between moderate and conservative clerics prevents Iran from fully developing its oil industry.

Unlike most producer countries, which try to maximize their oil output and operate at full capacity, Saudi Arabia

pumps oil at well below its maximum rate. By turning the taps on full, the output of oil could be increased from the OPEC **quota** of about 8 million barrels (1.3 million m^3) a day to 10 million barrels (1.6 million m^3) a day. To increase oil production in Iran or Iraq to that amount will require years of investment. While Saudi Arabia supplied less than 15 percent of U.S. oil imports in the late 1990s, it remains the most important supplier because of its low production costs and huge reserves. It is believed that one trillion barrels (160 billion m^3) of oil may eventually be recovered from Saudi Arabia's oil fields.

THE MAJOR COMPANIES IN THE OIL INDUSTRY

The world's largest oil companies grow even larger in the past few years as they embarked on a series of mergers. The largest deals were the $81 billion merger of Exxon and Mobil in 1999; the BP-Amoco merger in April 2000; the mergers of Chevron and Texaco in 2001 and Phillips and Conoco in 2002; and the deals that gave rise to the French giant TotalFinaElf in 1999 and 2000. The largest companies in oil services and refinery and oil rig construction are the French **multinational** Schlumberger plus U.S.-owned giants Baker Hughes, Bechtel, and Halliburton.

Big Oil: The Majors (2005)

	Revenues ($ billion)	Net profit ($ billion)
ExxonMobil	334.63	36.67
Royal Dutch/Shell Group	265.19	18.54
BP	249.47	22.63
ChevronTexaco	200.12	15.42
Total	144.94	14.51

After more than 3 decades of Ba'ath party rule, Iraq's future is uncertain, as a result of the March 2003 invasion and the removal of Saddam Hussein. With Hussein no longer in power, a Coalition Provisional Authority (CPA), led by the United States and Great Britain, was responsible for governing the country until an election could be held.

The election occurred on January 30, 2005. Its purpose was to elect individuals to the National Assembly. The purpose of the assembly is to create and approve a new constitution for Iraq. Upon the completion of the constitution, the National Assembly will be dissolved to make way for a new government. In the meantime, foreign bodies, including the U.S.-led Office of Reconstruction and Humanitarian Assistance (ORHA), the U.S. Army Corps of Engineers, private contractors, nongovernmental organizations, and coalition military forces, will remain involved in the rebuilding of the country.

Iraq has more than 112 billion barrels (18 billion m³) of proved oil reserves and possibly much more undiscovered oil in unexplored areas of the country. It is estimated that Iraq also contains at least 110 trillion cubic feet (17 trillion m³) of natural gas. Although not a central motivating factor for the

---

Iraq's future is uncertain after more than 3 decades of Ba'ath party rule.

U.S.-led military intervention —the Bush administration's case for war was based on the threat of terrorism and weapons of mass destruction—many people think oil played a significant role in the decision to remove Saddam Hussein from power. Saddam had repeatedly threatened the free flow of oil from the Persian Gulf area. This was dramatically illustrated when Iraqi troops occupied oil-rich Kuwait in 1990 and 1991. The occupation of Kuwait led to the 1991 Gulf War, which included troops from Arab and western countries. Some experts point out that if Iraq had built a nuclear weapon, it would have been hard to deter Saddam from attempting to control the Gulf region and the world oil market.

In 2003, the CPA estimated that it would cost $1.144 billion to rebuild Iraq's oil sector to its pre-war state and take 9 months to finish the project. Attacks on the 4,350-mile (7,000 km) long pipeline system and the 11,184-mile (18,000 km) long electric grid have hindered the reconstruction of Iraq's oil industry and affected Iraqi oil revenues.

These attacks fall into two distinct categories. The first category involves criminal activity. Since the 2003 invasion, Iraq's oil infrastructure has been looted. Everything from field pumping stations to refineries have been targets for theft. Organized crime is also stealing Iraqi oil and smuggling it out of the country. Usually, this oil is taken to Iran and exported as Iranian oil.

The second category involves attacks from groups that oppose the presence of U.S.

KEY CONCEPTS

Petrodollars is the term used to describe the money paid to oil-producing countries, especially those in the Middle East, and deposited in western banks. In other words, it is the U.S. dollars earned from the sale of oil. Petrodollars depend on the sale price of oil as well as the volume being sold, which in turn depends on oil production. The overall world supply of oil and the world demand determine the market price for oil. A price determined by OPEC can be maintained only as long as there is sufficient demand to absorb the amount being supplied in world markets. If demand exceeds supply, oil will be sold at an even higher price than that determined by OPEC. The opposite holds true when an oil glut occurs. This is reflected in a drop in the price after a certain time lag, regardless of the price dictated by OPEC.

and coalition troops, and the involvement of UN agencies.

In addition to attacks on its oil infrastructure, Iraq's oil industry is affected by years of centralized, state-run management, lack of investment, and inadequate maintenance of the oil fields. Although there has been a lack of money needed to rectify these long-term problems and rebuild the oil industry, oil production will remain slow until Iraq's vast oil infrastructure is protected from criminal and terrorist activities.

In spite of attacks on its oil infrastructure, Iraq's crude oil production is rising, with most of this oil production coming from the southern oil fields. Production in the northern oil fields has been hindered by bomb attacks on pipelines and other facilities. The U.S.-led coalition blamed these attacks on Ba'ath party loyalists and Islamic militants.

The wholesale destruction of oil wells did not occur during the early stages of the U.S.-led occupation of Iraq. However, the deteriorating security situation in Iraq after the end of major hostilities and an increase in terrorist activities in neighboring countries such as Saudi Arabia affected the oil market in 2003.

■■■ After years of rule by Saddam Hussein, more than 231 parties ran in the Iraqi general elections of 2005.

Oil and the Middle East

Many Middle East oil fields are easy to access, while those that are still productive in other parts of the world tend to be in less accessible environments, such as Siberia, tropical forests, or under the sea. Arabian oil is often relatively close to the surface in barren land. This makes Arabian oil fields ideal for development. Also, the pipelines that carry oil across Middle East deserts require only minimal maintenance because of dry desert conditions.

As far as oil is concerned, Saudi Arabia is the key country in the Middle East because it has vast, easily accessible resources. The frontiers of Saudi Arabia were created in the 1920s with the help of Great Britain, which supported the efforts of Ibn Saud to unify the Arabian peninsula. Set up as a kingdom, Saudi Arabia is similar to a family business. Decision making is concentrated in a handful of Saud clan leaders, and the best jobs are distributed among several thousand junior princes. The United States. has had a special relationship with the Saud family since Standard Oil won the concession for oil development in 1933. Surrounded by populous and powerful countries, the Saud

■■■ **Although the United States promised to remove all of its troops from Saudi Arabia following the first Gulf War, about 5,000 troops remained. Today, almost all of the troops have been removed.**

clan has been protected by the U.S. government. Similar arrangements have been put in place for other oil-rich Gulf states that are also ruled by **autocratic** cliques.

Saudi Arabia and the five other members of the Gulf Cooperation Council—Bahrain, Kuwait, Oman, Qatar, and the United Arab Emirates—are dominated by family sheikdoms. Together, these countries control about 45 percent of the world's proved oil reserves and a much higher percentage of easily accessible, cheap oil. Despite some moves toward greater democracy, popular discontent is growing.

Oil wealth has enabled Saudi authorities to reduce popular discontent by paying for hospitals, schools, roads, and mosques and by looking after the holy Islam cities of Mecca and Medina. However, Saudi Arabia's strongly conservative brand of Islam—Wahhabism—has been at odds with the westernization of Arabia, and this conservative brand of Islam has spawned a more militant form of Islam. Some Saudi individuals have used their oil wealth to support **Islamist** groups abroad. The U.S. government was shocked to discover that many of the people involved in the September 11, 2001, terrorist attacks were Saudi nationals, including Osama bin Laden. Much has changed since 9/11, and the United States has been reassessing its strategic priorities in all kinds of ways, including dependence on the oil of a potentially unstable Saudi Arabia.

The situation in Saudi Arabia is similar to the situation that existed in Iran in 1978. At that time, the Shah of Iran was toppled in a popular uprising.

> ### The situation in Saudi Arabia is similar to the situation that existed in Iran in 1978.

The West, which had counted on Iran's oil and its military support in the war against communism, was caught by surprise. Russia promptly invaded Afghanistan in order to ensure continuing control of its southern republics, where oil and gas resources were known to be plentiful and Islamic fundamentalism was growing. Middle East oil money was used to finance *mujaheddin* fighters in Afghanistan. These fighters included many Arabs opposed to foreigners, whether communist or capitalist. The collapse of the Soviet Union changed the global energy scene by opening up the FSU to western companies and bringing new competition to Middle East oil suppliers.

In the 1930s, Royal Dutch/Shell, BP (known at the time as Anglo-Persian), and French and U.S. oil companies were the key players in the Middle East. Oil had to be sold to the West because no one else could afford to buy it. Early oil rights in these countries were signed over to U.S., British, and French countries on very advantageous terms. After World War II, nationalist movements brought oil assets under local government control.

PERSIAN GULF DOMINATION OF GLOBAL OIL (2003)

Natural gas 35%

Excess oil production 90%

Oil production 25%

Oil production capacity 32%

Oil reserves 66%

| 0 | 10 | 20 | 30 | 40 | 50 | 60 | 70 | 80 | 90 | 100 |

PERCENT

Source: The Energy Information Administration (EIA)

However, the multinational oil companies were able to retain substantial influence in the Middle East oil business as a result of their technical know-how and financial clout.

Today, the global market for oil is much different, and many developing countries are buyers. The Russians, the Chinese, and the Japanese are as active in the battle for Middle East oil as the the traditional U.S., British, and French companies.

The shape of countries in the Middle East was largely determined by European countries after the collapse of the Ottoman Empire. Iraq, under British mandate, was a combination of three Ottoman provinces—Basra, Baghdad, and Mosul. This combination forced Kurds to share a country with Shi'ite and Sunni Arabs. The discovery by British prospectors of large oil deposits at Kirkuk in 1927 increased Iraq's strategic importance.

Middle East countries have spent little on developing domestic or cross-border infrastructures for water and energy supply.

The Kurds, the world's largest ethnic group without a state, have long considered the oil fields of northern Iraq as part of their homeland—Kurdistan. The war in Iraq might give the Kurds a chance to implement their claim, but the formal creation of a new Kurdish state would be fiercely opposed by Turkey and Iran, which have large Kurdish minorities. The potential for Iraq to fragment is increased by the presence of large, undeveloped oil fields in the Shi'ite-dominated south of the country.

Iran's economic progress has been severely hampered by the sanctions placed on its oil industry by the U.S. policy of containment, which aims to weaken Iran through strict economic sanctions and diplomatic isolation. Iran's inclusion in President George W. Bush's axis of evil looks unreasonable to some people, but many countries have been wary of doing deals with Iran

KEY CONCEPTS

Ottoman Empire The foundation for the Ottoman Empire was established by Osman I in 1301. When Sultan Mehmed II conquered Constantinople in 1453, the state grew into an empire. The Empire reached its height under Suleiman the Magnificent in the sixteenth century, when it stretched from the Persian Gulf in the east to Hungary in the northwest and from Egypt in the south to the Caucasus in the north. After its defeat at the Battle of Vienna in 1683, however, the empire began a slow decline, culminating in the defeat of the empire by the Allies in World War I.

Wahhabism For more than two centuries, Wahhabism has been Saudi Arabia's dominant faith. It is an austere form of Islam that insists on a literal interpretation of the Koran. Strict Wahhabis believe that all those who do not practice their form of Islam are heathens and enemies. Critics say that Wahhabism's rigidity has led it to misinterpret and distort Islam, pointing to extremists such as Osama bin Laden. Wahhabism's explosive growth began in the 1970s when Saudi charities started funding Wahhabi schools, or *madrassas*, and mosques from Islamabad to Culver City, California. Throughout its history, the Wahhabis have fiercely opposed any change or modernization that deviates from the fundamental teachings of the Koran. The telephone, radio broadcasts, and public education for women were once condemned in Saudi Arabia as innovations created by the Devil. Riots occurred in Saudi Arabia when television was introduced in 1965. These riots were quelled only after police fired on demonstrators. Similar tensions exist today. A recent ruling suggested that the music played when a mobile phone rings should be outlawed on religious grounds.

The Ras Tanura is the principal petroleum terminal in the Persian Gulf located in eastern Saudi Arabia.

in case it affects trade with the United States. Even so, both western and Asian oil and gas companies have signed big contracts with Iran.

Israel's location complicates the export routes of Arab producer countries because they are reluctant to trade with Israel. However, Israel is a major importer of energy because it has few fossil fuel resources, although offshore gas was discovered in recent years.

In the 1990s, when a Palestinian peace deal seemed to be emerging, Israel and Egypt joined forces to build a $1.3 billion refinery in Alexandria. The refinery is the largest Arab-Israel joint venture in the Middle East, and it began operations in April 2001. However, the changing political situation led Israel to sell its 20 percent share in the project to the National Bank of Egypt. As with the Israel-Egypt venture, many other regional projects that could improve the living standards of millions of people living in the Middle East have been frustrated by the political problems that plague the region.

Middle East countries have not spent their petrodollars wisely. Much of their income has gone to buy weapons or into investments overseas. They have spent little on developing domestic or cross-border infrastructures for water and energy supplies. They have spent even less on building democratic civil societies. High birth rates and low economic growth have reduced living standards and created large groups of jobless youths in a region where half the population is under the age of 15. The unresolved issues of Palestinian and Kurdish statehood and perceived U.S. double standards regarding Israel add to discontent and could eventually lead to regime change in the autocratic Gulf states.

The United States spent $440 billion on their military in 2004.

OIL AND MILITARY SPENDING

Defense contracts have formed an important part of the Middle East's trading relationship with the outside world. Saudi Arabia has bought more than $100 billion worth of U.S. weapons since 1974. Iran was the other twin pillar of U.S. strategy in the Middle East until 1978. Under the Shah, Iran was supplied with a vast array of fighter planes, tanks, air defense systems, and so forth. Iraq was also favored with western arms, especially during the 1980s when it was fighting a war with Iran. Turkey and Egypt, two other key players in the region, have bought large amounts of U.S. military equipment. British, French, and Russian suppliers have also been heavily involved in the buildup of arms in the Middle East. The Yamana contracts with Saudi Arabia were the biggest in British defense industry history (worth more than $100 billion over 20 years).

Arms Exports to Middle East	
(Year)	**($ billion)**
1964–1973	09.4
1974–1978	29.0
1979–1983	65.3
1984–1988	89.1
1989–1993	83.6
1994–1998	83.1

Source: U.S. Arms Control and Disarmament Agency, International Institute for Strategic Studies, etc.

Understanding Global Issues—The Battle for Oil

Born: about 1880, in Riyadh, Saudi Arabia
Died: November 8, 1953, at Taif, Saudi Arabia
Legacy: Restored the Arabian state of his ancestors, founded the Kingdom of Saudi Arabia, and ensured its prosperity.

Navigate to **www.saudinf.com/ main/b42.htm** for more information about Ibn Saud. Also click on **www.saudinf.com** for more information about Saudi Arabia.

People in Focus

Abdul-Aziz ibn Abdul-Rahman Al Saud, or Ibn Saud as he was known in the West, was Saudi Arabia's first king. During his reign of more than 50 years, Saud oversaw the transformation of his impoverished country into a major oil exporter. This dramatic success was due in large part to his skillful use of traditional sources of power in Arabia—family and tribal loyalties and the strict tenets of Islam.

Saud spent his childhood as a "penniless exile" in Kuwait after his family's lands were occupied by Ottoman troops. His family's lands were in the Nejd, a vast plateau in central Saudi Arabia. Saudi Arabia's capital city, Riyadh, is located in the Nejd.

He became the leader of the Saud dynasty in 1901 at the age of 21, with the title Sultan of Nejd. At that time, he began work to reclaim his family's lands. He accomplished this in 1902, with a small army of relatives and servants. By 1912, he had completed his conquest of the Nejd and organized a well-trained army. He changed the name of his kingdom to Saudi Arabia in 1932 after securing his power over the majority of the Arabian peninsula.

Oil was discovered in Saudi Arabia in 1938. These oil deposits proved to be among the richest in the world. Saud's subsequent decision to grant sizeable control of the oil fields to U.S. oil companies led to the U.S.-directed development of Saudi Arabia's oil deposits and created close ties to the United States. When World War II led the United States into the Middle East, Saud was the Arab leader President Franklin Roosevelt most wanted to meet. The royal family profited the most from the early revenues of the oil boom. As the revenue grew, however, Saud began to spend some of the money on national improvements.

Mapping Oil

ARCTIC OCEAN

PACIFIC OCEAN

5.0%

NORTH ATLANTIC OCEAN

Figure 1: The World of Oil
The Middle East has the largest proved oil reserves, production, and **spare capacity**. The United States is the largest importer, refiner, and consumer of oil. Oil powers 97 percent of transport in the United States. The U.S. oil industry employs 1.5 million people, operates nearly 190,000 service stations, and maintains about 932,000 miles (1.5 million km) of oil and gas pipelines. Oil is not the only cause of trouble in the conflicts represented on the map, but it does play a part.

PANAMA CANAL

8.6%

PACIFIC OCEAN

N

0	1000	2000	3000	miles
0	1,609	3,219	4,828	kilometers

SCALE AT EQUATOR

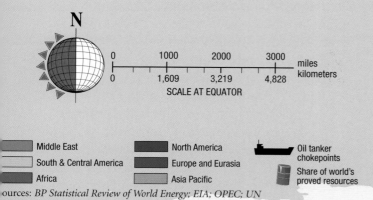

▢ Middle East	▢ North America	▬ Oil tanker chokepoints
▢ South & Central America	▢ Europe and Eurasia	▢ Share of world's proved resources
▢ Africa	▢ Asia Pacific	

Sources: *BP Statistical Review of World Energy; EIA; OPEC; UN*

ARCTIC OCEAN

★ BALTIC

11.7%

★ BOSPHORUS

SUEZ CANAL

★ STRAIT OF HORMUZ

BAB AL-MANDAB
(RED SEA)

9.5%

61.9%

PACIFIC
OCEAN

3.4%

★ MALACCA STRAIT

ATLANTIC
OCEAN

INDIAN
OCEAN

Figure 2: Leading importers of crude oil (thousand barrels per day in 2004)

USA	10,771	France	1,711
Japan	4,250	Italy	1,744
S. Korea	2,283	India	1,943
Germany	2,212	Spain	1,188

Figure 3: Leading oil producers (thousand barrels per day in 2004)

FSU	10,581	UAE	2,344
Saudi Arabia	8,897	Canada	1,405
USA	5,430	Nigeria	2,357
Iran	3,834	Kuwait	2,289
China	3,485	Great Britain	1,843
Mexico	3,383	Brazil	1,477
Norway	2,797	Iraq	2,106
Venezuela	3,009		

ANTARCTICA

Charting Oil

Figure 4: Proved Oil Reserves—Total 1,144,013 *(million barrels at the end of 2004)*

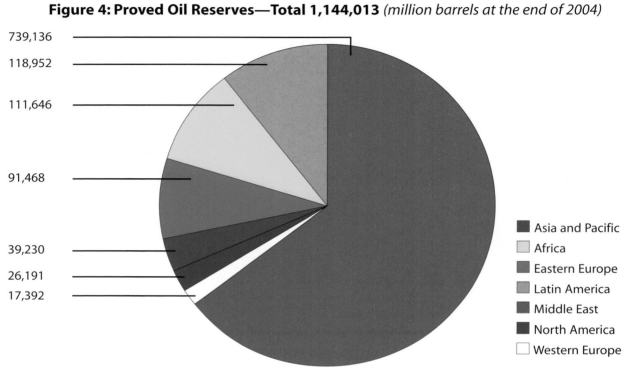

739,136
118,952
111,646
91,468
39,230
26,191
17,392

- ■ Asia and Pacific
- ▨ Africa
- ▨ Eastern Europe
- ▨ Latin America
- ▨ Middle East
- ■ North America
- □ Western Europe

Source: OPEC Annual Statistical Bulletin 2004

Figure 5: Crude Oil Production—Total 70,575 *(thousand barrels per day in 2004)*

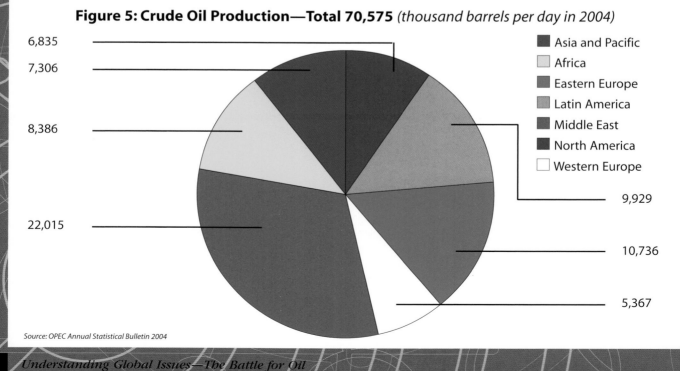

- ■ Asia and Pacific
- □ Africa
- ▨ Eastern Europe
- ▨ Latin America
- ▨ Middle East
- ■ North America
- □ Western Europe

6,835
7,306
8,386
22,015

9,929
10,736
5,367

Source: OPEC Annual Statistical Bulletin 2004

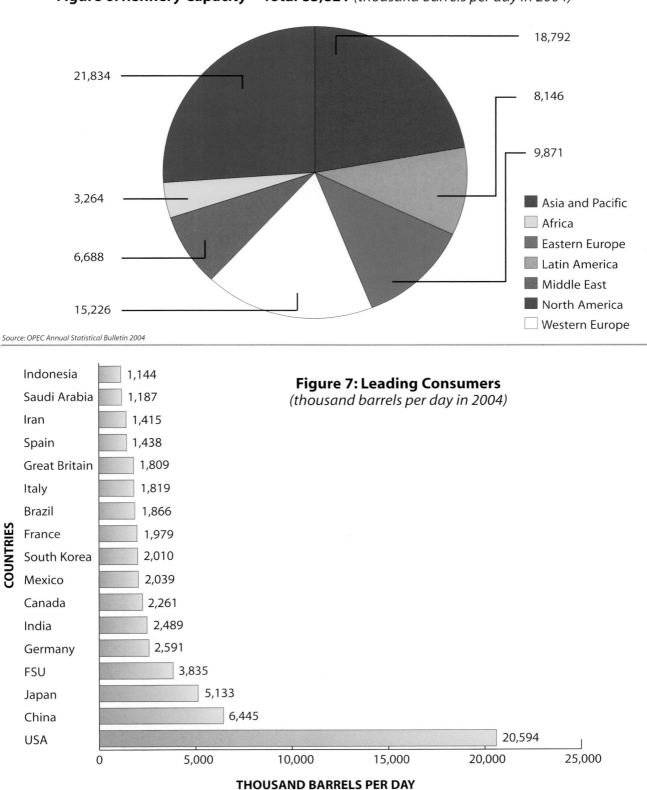

Figure 6: Refinery Capacity—Total 83,821 *(thousand barrels per day in 2004)*

18,792

8,146

9,871

■ Asia and Pacific
□ Africa
■ Eastern Europe
▨ Latin America
▩ Middle East
■ North America
□ Western Europe

21,834

3,264

6,688

15,226

Source: OPEC Annual Statistical Bulletin 2004

Figure 7: Leading Consumers
(thousand barrels per day in 2004)

COUNTRIES	THOUSAND BARRELS PER DAY
Indonesia	1,144
Saudi Arabia	1,187
Iran	1,415
Spain	1,438
Great Britain	1,809
Italy	1,819
Brazil	1,866
France	1,979
South Korea	2,010
Mexico	2,039
Canada	2,261
India	2,489
Germany	2,591
FSU	3,835
Japan	5,133
China	6,445
USA	20,594

Source: OPEC Annual Statistical Bulletin 2004

Beyond the Middle East

After Saudi Arabia, Russia is the world's largest producer and exporter of crude oil. At the beginning of the twentieth century, Russia produced half the world's oil from its oil fields in the Caspian Sea area. Under Soviet rule, however, this region remained poorly developed. Since 1990, the oil and gas fields of Central Asia have come to be seen as the world's largest untapped reservoir of hydrocarbons. Even

so, the Caspian and Siberian fields are not as large as those in the Middle East, and they are far more expensive to develop. Proved oil reserves in the FSU in 2002 were only one tenth of those in the Middle East. Since 1990, however, Russia has become a key supplier of oil and gas to Europe and Israel.

Russia pumps more than 7 million barrels (11 billion m^3) a day, mainly from West Siberian fields such as Samatlor. Develop-

ment of other large oil fields in East Siberia, the Caspian Sea area, and Sakhalin is taking place. Under communism, the oil industry was state-owned, and despite privatization during the 1990s, state monopolies still have a major influence on Russia's oil industry. All of Russia's oil pipelines, for example, are run by state-owned Transneft, the world's largest crude oil transportation company. Gazprom, of which

▬▬▬ The large oil reserves in the Northern Caspian Sea area will be difficult to recover. These reserves are deep underground, laced with poisonous hydrogen sulfide and are under very high pressure.

38 percent is owned by the Russian government, controls both gas production and pipeline distribution.

Russia is heavily dependent on oil and gas for both foreign earnings and domestic revenues. Taxes paid by Gazprom alone account for 25 percent of the Russian government's annual revenues. In other words, oil and gas are critical components of Russia's economy. Russia's fortunes are closely tied to energy prices and the market rate for oil in particular. An oil price below $20 a barrel ($126/m^3) would seriously affect Russia's federal budget.

Development of the Russian oil industry has been hampered by years of underinvestment. Although western oil companies showed strong interest in the FSU after 1990, the combination of political risk, legal uncertainty, and Russian **nationalism** have meant that foreign investment has been minimal. In the meantime, Russian companies such as Yukos, Sibneft, and Lukoil, helped by the high oil prices of recent years, have emerged as serious players in international markets. However, output from West Siberia appears to have peaked, and in order to maintain production, new investment is urgently needed. The question of foreign involvement is likely to become more pressing. In early 2003, BP announced the biggest western oil investment in the FSU so far—a $6.75 billion deal involving joint ownership of TNK and Sidanco.

Although most Soviet oil was in Russia, some of the other newly independent states of the FSU, especially around the Caspian Sea, have great hydrocarbon potential. Five states—Russia, Azerbaijan, Kazakhstan, Turkmenistan, and Iran—border the Caspian Sea and share its hydrocarbon deposits. However, after a decade of argument, there is still no

---

At the beginning of the twentieth century, Russia produced half the world's oil from its oil fields in the Caspian Sea area.

---

agreement among all of these countries about legal entitlements. In these countries, foreign investors have been competing with the Russians for stakes in the oil and gas industry. On the one hand, longstanding personal links and the physical infrastructure put in place by Moscow, such as pipelines and refineries, favor the Russians. On the other hand, the newly independent states are keen to bring in as much foreign money as possible, without giving up control of their oil and gas resources.

Sparsely populated and with relatively undeveloped economies, these countries want to sell their oil and gas on world markets. However, the markets lie far away, for example, in China, Europe, India, Japan, and the United States. Since the region is also landlocked, the only cost-effective way to transport the oil and gas to market is to carry it by pipeline to user countries or to ports where it can be loaded onto tankers for shipment. Pipeline routes have become the cause of much political wrangling.

Russia has been pushing the claims of its major Black Sea terminal at Novorossiisk. Others have proposed a variety of routes that are independent of Russia.

THE ADDED VALUE MARKET

Most refining capacity and downstream activities are controlled by the oil majors. ExxonMobil has a refining capacity of more than 6 million barrels (1 million m^3) a day, almost twice as much as its nearest rivals Royal Dutch/Shell, BP, and PDVSA, and as much as all of the Persian Gulf producers combined. This domination of the "added value" market enabled the five oil majors to make net profits of $180 billion in the 5-year period 1997 to 2001.

Options are reduced by the messy politics of the Caucasus and U.S. opposition to trans-Iranian routes. Turkey also has an interest, since tanker traffic across the Black Sea passes through the narrow straits of the Bosphorus on its way to overseas markets. Turkey is worried about dangerous congestion in the seaways near Istanbul. It supported construction of the 1,094-mile (1,760-km) pipeline from the Caspian Sea area to the Mediterranean port of Ceyhan. The pipeline began operating in 2005. The Baku-Tbilisi-Ceyhan Pipeline Company (BTC) is owned by several shareholders. They include BP, which owns 38.21 percent; the Azerbaijan state oil company SOCAR, which owns 25 percent; Norway's Statoil, which owns 9.58 percent; and Unocal, with 8.9 percent.

In late 2002, political agreement was reached for a 932-mile (1,500 km) pipeline to bring gas from Turkmenistan across Afghanistan to the Pakistan coast, although no foreign investors had yet been identified with the project.

Latin America pumps more oil toward the United States than any other part of the world. Mexico, Venezuela, Colombia, and Ecuador generate more than one third of U.S. oil imports.

The United States makes up roughly 5 percent of the world's population, but it consumes 25 percent of its oil. Because of this need for oil, the United States buys oil from suppliers around the world. Although the largest oil reserves are in the Middle East, for the time being,

■■■■ **The BTC pipeline will transport 50 million tons (45 million t) of crude oil per year from Azerbaijan's capital, Baku, to the new Mediterranean terminal at the port of Ceyhan.**

the United States depends more on Latin American oil than it does on Middle Eastern oil.

The discovery of oil reserves in Latin America was expected to raise the standard of living in countries such as Mexico and Venezuela. For Latin Americans who live in the shadow of the United States, economic independence was finally a realistic goal.

In 1938, Mexico nationalized its oil industry. This move created hopes for a better life and resulted in a wave of patriotism. In Venezuela, which helped create OPEC in 1960, high oil prices in the 1970s brought large amounts of cash into the country and led to ambitious development plans. In Ecuador, the discovery of oil offered the country a way to escape the instability of the agriculture market.

For the most part, Latin America's oil producers have societies that are more modern, and have larger middle classes, better infrastructures, and better education systems than Latin American countries that do not produce oil. However, these countries have not developed as far or as fast as expected. Instead, Latin American oil-producing countries have experienced corruption, political instability, environmental devastation, and social inequality. While these

---

In Mexico, the world's fifth-largest oil producer, almost 45 percent of the country lives in poverty.

---

problems are not caused just by the presence of oil resources, some people believe these problems may be a side effect of owning one of the world's most coveted natural resources.

In Venezuela, the dreams of a better standard of living for its citizens were dashed in the 1980s. As a result of a decrease in the price of oil and excessive government spending, the country accumulated a large debt and began to experience civil unrest.

In Mexico, the world's fifth-largest oil producer, almost 45 percent of the country lives in poverty, and the country's proved oil reserves are in decline. Even if Mexico succeeds in attracting foreign investment for new oil projects—which will be difficult because foreign oil companies have not been allowed to operate in Mexico since 1938—the country will still have to deal with increasing poverty and ongoing corruption at PEMEX, the state-run oil company.

In Ecuador, oil development has resulted in serious damage to the country's Amazon forests. It has disrupted the lives of thousands of Amazonian Natives, and it has spawned a resistance movement that is determined to stop further oil development in Ecuador's Amazon forests.

In Peru, officials are trying to convince a wary public that developing its natural gas deposits in the Amazon will benefit future generations. However, this has not been the case in Ecuador and other Amazon countries. In Brazil, citizens and advocacy groups are campaigning for the use of alternative fuels, such as natural gas and sunflower oil.

KEY CONCEPTS

The Caspian Sea covers 144,000 square miles (373,000 sq km). It is the world's largest lake. It is bordered on the northeast by Kazakhstan, on the southeast by Turkmenistan, on the south by Iran, on the southwest by Azerbaijan, and on the northwest by Russia. The Caspian's surface lies 92 feet (28 m) below sea level. It is 3,200 feet (980 m) deep in the south; the shallow northern half averages about 17 feet (5 m). The Caspian Sea is fed by the Volga River, which supplies more than 75 percent of its water. The rest of the water is supplied by the Ural, Emba, Kura, and Terek rivers. All of this water stays in the Caspian Sea because it has no outlet.

When oil was first discovered in Ecuador, it was seen as the country's salvation from poverty.

In Colombia, leftist guerrillas and right-wing **paramilitaries** are stealing oil and gas from pipelines. These attacks on the oil and gas industry are fueling an armed conflict that has plagued this country for decades.

To make matters worse, three of the top four Latin American suppliers to the United States—Mexico, Colombia, and Ecuador—could stop exporting oil due to declining reserves within the next 10 to 15 years. Although some people believe new discoveries will significantly extend the life of Latin American oil exports, sooner or later, the United States will have to obtain most of its oil imports from the Middle East.

Since it is possible that the bulk of Latin American oil exports will end in the not too distant future, it seems quite probable that oil was an important consideration when the United States decided to intervene militarily in Iraq. In addition to the energy security offered by Iraq's 112 billion barrels (18 billion m^3) of proved oil reserves, the second-largest known reserves in the world, at current prices, Iraqi oil is worth $3 trillion.

The U.S. occupation of Iraq is also consistent with the 2002 U.S. energy plan that emphasizes energy security as a key element of its. foreign policy.

The United States is also talking about the possibility of Iraq leaving OPEC and renegotiating pre-war contracts it signed with France and Russia. As the Energy Intelligence Group, publishers of the industry bible, *Petroleum Intelligence Weekly*, points out, "The war in Iraq is over. Now it's time for business."

Regardless of its reasons for occupying Iraq, oil and those countries that produce it will continue to be the focus of U.S. foreign policy.

Petroleum Engineer

Duties: Plans and supervises oil and gas drilling operations. Designs equipment and most profitable means of oil and gas retrieval. Plans and supervises well operation and maintenance.
Education: Undergraduate degree in engineering, geology, geophysics, tectonics, or mining
Interests: Travel, engineering, and high-risk activities

Navigate to the Society of Petroleum Engineers website **www.spe.org** for more information about a career as a petroleum engineer.

Careers in Focus

Petroleum engineers are involved in all phases of oil exploration, from choosing the prospective site to taking down the drilling rig after extracting the oil. According to petroleum engineers, it is a gambler's life. Those who do well in this high-risk field are attracted to taking risks and engineering.

The typical petroleum engineer works in the field. First, prospective sites that have a strong likelihood of containing oil or gas are scouted. Then, samples are taken from the site to determine the amount and quality of oil, the depth at which these resources lie, and the equipment that will be needed to properly extract them. The petroleum engineer supervises construction and operations at the site. Finally, when the well or pocket is exhausted, the petroleum engineer supervises the removal of the drilling equipment and the safe return of the land to structural stability and oversees the removal of any waste left at the site.

Although petroleum engineers spend most of their time in the field, they also rely heavily on computer models to simulate the effects of various drilling options.

Petroleum engineers must be able to identify, analyze, and solve problems; communicate well, both orally and in writing; have an aptitude for computing and design; and be practical and creative.

Threats to the Oil Supply

A complex transportation and storage system has been developed to move oil from the oil field to the refinery and then to the service station. Every day, tens of millions of barrels (m^3) of oil are transported through a worldwide system of pipelines, tankers, and trucks. This system is an easy target for terrorists.

More than half the oil consumed in the United States is imported and transported by pipelines, tankers, and trucks. As a result, terrorist groups such as al-Qaeda can disrupt the free flow of crude oil into the United States by attacking oil transportation routes. Attacking the oil transportation system and disrupting oil imports could have a significant impact on the price of oil and the global economy.

Terrorist groups have already tried to attack oil tankers in the Persian Gulf and near the Horn of Africa. In 2002, members of al-Qaeda were suspected of planning attacks against British and U.S. ships and tankers passing through the Strait of Gibraltar. They were arrested by the Moroccan government. However, terrorists have

■■■ **The United States has more than 141,509 miles (227,736 km) of railway that transport oil across the country.**

successfully carried out some attacks. In 2002, al-Qaeda used a boat packed with explosives to badly damage a French supertanker off Yemen. After this attack, many people thought it

---

Tankers and pipelines are easy targets for terrorists.

---

was possible that terrorists might seize a ship and crash it into another vessel or into a refinery or port.

Al-Qaeda has made it clear that it plans to hurt the West economically by attacking the world's oil transportation system. These attacks would disrupt life in the West, but more important, serious interruptions in the flow of oil might result in the overthrow of Persian Gulf monarchies that depend on oil revenues for their survival.

Tankers and pipelines are easy targets for terrorists. Tankers are slow and cannot maneuver quickly enough to avoid terrorist attacks such as the one that damaged the French tanker. Also, they have no protection, and on the high seas, there is no place to hide. There are approximately 3,300 tankers, including about 300 supertankers, involved in the global oil trade. These tankers are susceptible to attacks on

the high seas or while passing through narrow straits in areas such as the Persian Gulf and Southeast Asia. Oil tankers are forced to pass through one or more of three narrow straits—the entrances to the Red Sea and the Persian Gulf, and the Straits of Malacca between Indonesia and Malaysia. Half of all oil shipments bound for East Asia and two-thirds of global liquefied natural gas shipments pass through the Straits of Malacca. These three straits are controlled by Muslim countries where terrorists are known to operate. These straits are very narrow, and a single burning supertanker could easily block these waterways. Such an event could affect the global oil market for several weeks.

Pipelines carry about 40 percent of the world's oil. Due to their length, pipelines are very difficult to protect. This makes pipelines potential targets for terrorists. A simple explosive device can puncture a pipeline and put it out of commission. In 2001, for example, terrorists attempted to sabotage an oil pipeline that supplies Saudi Arabia's Ras Tanura terminal, which handles 5 million barrels (800,000 m^3) of oil a day. This attack could have seriously affected the global oil market.

The threat of terrorist attacks against the oil transportation system has had an impact on oil prices. For example, the cost to insure tankers traveling through dangerous waters has increased dramatically. Insurance rates for tankers passing through Yemeni waters have tripled since the attack on the French tanker. The insurance rates for a typical supertanker carrying about 2 million barrels (300,000 m^3) of oil rose from $150,000 to $450,000 a trip. This increase added about 15 cents a barrel to the cost of the oil. In addition, insurance rates have increased for pipelines and oil terminals. These rate increases have also added to the price of oil.

Threats to the security of the oil supply are not new. As a result of the 1973 Middle East oil embargo, the Iranian Revolution, and the Soviet invasion of Afghanistan, the United States took a hard stand on oil security. In his last State of the Union address in January 1980, President Jimmy Carter stated that any "attempt by an outside force to gain control of the Persian Gulf region will be regarded as an assault on the vital interests of the United States," and he promised to defend that interest by "any means necessary, including military force."

Five weeks after Carter's speech, the U.S. military established the United States Rapid Deployment Joint Task Force (RDJTF) at MacDill Air Force Base in Florida. When

President Jimmy Carter made clear in 1980 that Soviet aggression around the world threatened the free flow of Middle Eastern oil.

Ronald Reagan became president in January 1981, the RDJTF commanded 100,000 Army troops, 50,000 Marines, and additional Air Force and Navy personnel. In January 1983, the RDJTF became the U.S. Central Command (CENTCOM), which now commands and controls the U.S. military in 25 countries in Central and Southwest Asia, the Middle East, and Northeast Africa. Since the creation of CENTCOM more than 20 years ago, the U.S. military has positioned itself so that it can protect U.S. interests around the world.

In March 2001, Energy Secretary Spencer Abraham presented the Bush administration's National Energy Strategy. This strategy, which was "founded on the understanding that diversity of supply means security of supply," had actually been in place for more than 10 years. Although energy planners know it is not possible to replace the oil from Persian Gulf countries with oil from other countries, the United States has diversified the sources of its oil supply in order to reduce its dependence on Persian Gulf oil. These alternative oil suppliers have become strategically important to the United States, and there is a striking **correlation** between the

presence of oil and the global deployment of the U.S. military.

In recent years, many U.S. military operations have occurred in countries that possess oil. For example, in Somalia, just before pro-U.S. President Mohamed Siad Barre was overthrown in 1991, Conoco, Amoco, Chevron, and Phillips obtained oil concessions for nearly two-thirds of the country's territory. Fighting between clans began after the overthrow of Barre, and in 1992, the U.S. military launched Operation Restore Hope in an attempt to restore peace to Somalia. While the operation was initiated to help the many starving Somalis affected by

---

There is a striking correlation between the presence of oil and the global deployment of the U.S. military.

---

clan fighting, stability in the country would have enabled the oil companies to explore the country's potentially rich oil fields.

In the Caspian Sea region, which may contain 200 billion (32 billion m^3) barrels of oil, the U.S. military has been fighting terrorism and trying to secure possible oil pipeline routes. In 2001, the United States gave $4.4 million in military aid to Azerbaijan. This aid was intended to help Azerbaijan combat terrorism, promote peace in the region, and open up transportation and trade corridors. Azeri President Heydar Aliyev said that providing security for the oil and gas pipelines was an important part of Azerbaijan's fight against terrorism

In 2001, the United States gave the country of Georgia $64 million in military aid and promised to send Special Forces advisers to train 2,000 Georgians in anti-terrorism techniques. According to the Georgian Defense Ministry, "Servicemen trained under the U.S. Train and Equip program might help provide security for the [Baku-Tblisi-Ceyhan oil] pipeline."

In 2002, the Bush administration sent Special Forces troops to Colombia to train Colombian troops to protect an Occidental Petroleum pipeline.

West Africa has more than 33 billion barrels (5 billion m^3) of proved oil reserves, supplies 15 percent of U.S. oil imports, and may supply 25 percent of U.S. imports by 2015. In June 2002, a report from the private African Oil Policy Initiative Group recommended that the United States consider setting up a base of operations in the area.

KEY CONCEPTS

The Carter Doctrine was the first U.S. Presidential public pronouncement since the Vietnam War of the possible commitment of U.S. troops to protect essential U.S. national interests. In so doing, the United States extended its military shield to the Persian Gulf region and, in effect, modified the Nixon Doctrine, which relied on U.S. allies in a region not only to defend themselves with U.S. aid, but to also protect U.S. regional interests. Carter's policy was designed to stop further Soviet aggression and to deter actions that might eventually expand ongoing conflicts in the Persian Gulf region.

DISRUPTION OF THE SUPPLY BY ISLAMIC EXTREMISTS

The governments in many Middle East oil-producing countries are at risk from Islamic extremists who want to gain control of these sources of oil. Control could come about through the overthrow of governments or through threats that secure the cooperation of governments. There would be worldwide economic consequences if Islamic extremists controlled some or all of the Middle East's oil reserves.

If Islamic extremists gained control of 8 million barrels (1.3 million m^3) of Arab OPEC oil a day, but not the supply from Saudi Arabia, Kuwait, the UAE, and Qatar, and cut output by 90 percent, about 10 percent of the world oil supply, or more than 7 million barrels (1.1 million m^3) a day, would be removed from the market. If OPEC countries used their spare capacity to and if Saudi Arabia, Kuwait, the UAE, and Qatar made up some of the supply cut, the reduction in world production would be limited to about 3.5 million barrels ($550{,}000$ m^3) a day.

Assume that Islamic extremists gained control of 8 million barrels (1.3 million m^3) of Arab OPEC oil a day and the Saudis and the rest of OPEC refused to make up any of the supply cut. The Saudis have been reluctant to fight terrorism. In addition, they have been disappointed in the way the Israeli-Palestinian conflict has been handled, and they are worried about Muslim extremists in their own country. If Saudi Arabia and the rest of the Arab OPEC countries chose not to make up the supply cut,

In 2004, Middle Eastern nations controlled nearly 65 percent of the world's oil reserves.

the market would lose 7 million barrels (1.1 million m^3) a day.

Assume that Islamic extremists gained control of the entire oil output of Arab Muslim nations and that they cut this production by 10 million barrels (1.6 million m^3) a day. Bin Laden and other extremists want to overthrow the Saudi monarchy and the other dynastic rulers in the region. Although a U.S. military occupation of the region could maintain oil supplies, it would be difficult to sustain. Furthermore, 10 million barrels (1.6 million m^3) a day could be lost as a result of damage to oil infrastructures and attacks against the oil transportation system.

The first case poses no serious problems. Oil from government reserves would offset most of the supply cut. In this case, oil prices would rise only few dollars per barrel, and gasoline prices would rise only a few cents per gallon. The second case, however, has important implications. Oil prices would rise dramatically, and North American gasoline prices would approach European levels. This increase in the price of oil would likely cause or deepen **recessions** in the United States and throughout the world. The third case would cause enormous economic problems. Oil prices would rise above $150 per barrel, and U.S. gasoline prices would increase two or three times their current price. An increase of this magnitude would plunge the United States into its worst recession since World War II.

Oil Well Firefighter

Duties: Extinguishes oil and gas well fires
Education: Generally must pass a written exam; tests of strength, physical stamina, coordination, and agility; and a medical examination that includes drug screening
Interests: Public service, danger

Navigate to
www.wildwell.com/ home.htm for information about how to cap a burning oil well.

Careers in Focus

Every year, fires and other emergencies take lives and destroy property. Firefighters help deal with these dangers daily and respond quickly to various emergencies. Oil well firefighters are a special type of firefighter.

Oil well firefighters played a crucial role after the Gulf War. When Saddam Hussein ordered the burning of more than 600 Kuwaiti oil wells in 1991, teams of oil well firefighters were sent in to put out the fires. Experts claimed it would take years to extinguish the fires, but firefighting teams completed the task in 9 months.

At best, this job is tough and risky. As no two oil well fires are alike, firefighters must use various procedures to battle the blaze. The procedure needed depends on the type of oil, the volume of oil flow, availability of water, and numerous other factors. Oil well firefighters must assess and evaluate the situation to determine the most effective way to combat the fire.

As oil well fires can be unpredictable and dangerous, courage, endurance, and strength are among the personal qualities oil well firefighters must possess. Mental alertness and mechanical aptitude are also necessary. Initiative and good judgment are extremely important because oil well firefighters must often make quick decisions in dangerous situations.

Oil and the Environment

The burning of fossil fuels—coal, oil, and gas—is blamed for environmental problems such as pollution and global warming. The environmental problems caused by oil entered the political debate in the 1980s, gathering ground with the 1992 Rio summit and mounting concerns over climate change. At first, the oil companies lobbied to counteract the anti-fossil fuel movement, but some changed their policies as evidence accumulated and public opinion hardened. BP and Shell were the first two major oil companies to accept their environmental responsibilities and take more account of environmental and social issues.

Although most oil companies are now investing heavily in renewable energy, their main business is still oil and gas. Meeting customer needs requires continuous exploration and development, sometimes in regions where ecosystems are fragile or the political regime controversial. Oil companies must now invest in local community projects and environmental protection as well as find and extract oil. Where profit margins are low,

> *The environmental problems caused by oil entered the political debate in the 1980s.*

such extra expenditure can make a project uneconomic.

Large-scale oil projects are becoming more difficult to justify in the eyes of a skeptical public. For example, it is claimed that burning the fuel carried by the Baku-Tbilisi-Ceyhan pipeline will contribute 187 million tons (170 million t) of carbon dioxide to global warming each year.

It is suggested that the entire 932-mile (1,500 km) pipeline will be a military zone and that construction will involve massive disruption of land and communities. Oil companies argue that the pipeline will be buried for most of its length, that it will be carefully routed to avoid villages and archaeological sites, and that the zone of disturbance will be less than 100 feet (30 m) wide. Moreover, the pipeline will avoid adding to the tanker traffic through the Bosphorus, where 4,500 tankers a year carry 66 million tons (60 million t) of oil through a narrow strait.

Although tanker accidents and spills are rare, tanker traffic will increase as Asia and the West import more oil. The development of oil fields in Russia, the Caspian Sea area, and Africa is bound to increase the risk. Tankers carrying Siberian oil through the icy waters of the Gulf of Finland or the Baltic are of particular concern. Yet tankers

KEY CONCEPTS

Kyoto Protocol was formally adopted by 84 countries in Kyoto, Japan, in 1997. The agreement gives industrialized countries until 2012 to reduce their greenhouse gas emissions. The United States renounced the treaty In 2001 due to cost. The Kyoto Protocol's future is far from assured as various nations have shown hesitation, due to perceived negative effects on their respective economies.

Rio Summit In 1992, leaders from 108 nations met in Rio de Janeiro, Brazil, to discuss, among other things, global warming. They agreed that human activities might be warming Earth more than was normal and that they should take action to reduce the production and emission of greenhouse gases.

are usually a cheaper way to transport oil than pipelines, so sea traffic will continue to increase.

According to the American Petroleum Institute (API), the U.S. oil industry is "a steward of the environment," spending $98 billion on environmental protection during the 1990s. The API points out that with the use of directional drilling, slimhole rigs, and other technological advances oil can be found with less disturbance to wetlands and other sensitive environments.

In spite of these claims, environmental legislation has often been resisted by both oil companies and the automobile industry. Oil company opposition to the Kyoto accord provoked an outpouring of public protest, including consumer boycotts. Although companies such as Shell have tried to present themselves as socially and environmentally responsible, it has been an uphill struggle to convince the public.

THE OIL INDUSTRY AND CLIMATE CHANGE

Many environmental activists see the thirst for oil as extremely damaging. They argue that the burning of fossil fuels causes pollution and global warming, and oil field development can damage local communities and ecosystems. There is bitter opposition to proposals to extend oil exploration in areas such as the Arctic National Wildlife Refuge. Commenting on the trans-Turkish pipeline, Friends of the Earth said, "In unlocking the Caspian Sea's fossil fuel reserves, the proposed Baku-Tbilisi-Ceyhan pipeline would become a key part of the system extracting carbon from beneath the Earth's surface and spewing it into the atmosphere, driving the process of climate change that in recent years has inflicted flooding, drought, and sea level rises on millions of people from Honduras to Mozambique and Bangladesh". Such talk exasperates oil industry executives, who point out that oil and gas provide convenient and affordable energy not only for large-scale manufacturing, but also for the comforts of everyday life. Yet there is no denying the growing attention that the oil industry has to pay to public concerns about the social and environmental impact of its activities. Public trust in big oil companies is not great, especially after disasters such as the Exxon Valdez tanker spill and Shell's mishandling of its operations in the Nigerian oil delta. Most of the public pressure is on U.S. and European companies. Newer oil companies have had less trouble because the public in developing countries is more concerned with economic hardship than with environmental issues.

■■■ **The Exxon Valdez oil spill cost Exxon Corp. a settlement of almost $1 billion USD for environmental violations.**

Timeline of Events

1859
Edwin Drake drills the first producing oil well in Titusville, Pennsylvania.

1870
John D. Rockefeller enters the oil refining business and forms Standard Oil to produce kerosene for lighting purposes.

1873
The Nobel family drills for oil in the Baku area in Russia, modern-day Azerbaijan.

1882
Thomas Edison invents the electric light bulb, endangering future oil markets.

1885
The petroleum industry is developed in Russia. The Royal Dutch oil company develops the oil industry in Sumatra, Indonesia.

1892
Marcus Samuel forms Shell oil company to transport petroleum through the Suez Canal.

1896
The invention of the automobile resurrects the market for oil.

1901
Oil is discovered in Persia, modern-day Iran. An oil well in Texas called Spindletop shoots oil 150 feet (46 m) into the air. The term *gusher* is coined to describe this event.

1903
California is the top oil-producing U.S. state.

1905
Oil is discovered in Oklahoma.

1907
Shell and Royal Dutch merge to form one oil company.

1910
Large-scale oil production begins in Mexico.

1911
Standard Oil is split into smaller oil companies such as Exxon, Mobil, Amoco, Sohio, and Chevron.

1922
Venezuela begins producing oil.

1927
Large deposits of oil are discovered in Iraq.

1933
Standard Oil of California, or Chevron, becomes heavily involved in drilling for oil in Saudi Arabia.

1938
Oil is discovered in Kuwait and Saudi Arabia.

1956
Oil is discovered in Algeria and Nigeria.

1959
Oil is discovered in Libya.

1960
OPEC is established.

■ In economic terms, the "real," or inflation adjusted, cost of gasoline in 2005 was 30 percent below the all-time average in the United States.

1968
Oil is discovered in Alaska, but it is not exploited until 1977.

1969
Oil is discovered in the North Sea, but it is not exploited until 1975.

1973
The first energy crisis occurs as a result of an Arab oil embargo against the United States in retaliation for U.S. support of Israel in the Yom Kippur war.

1979
The second energy crisis occurs as a result of the Iranian revolution, which causes major disruptions in oil supplies from the Persian Gulf.

1980
OPEC encounters trouble because two of its members, Iran and Iraq, are at war.

1982
OPEC establishes production quotas.

1990
The third energy crisis occurs when Iraq invades Kuwait, causing another major disruption in oil supplies from the Persian Gulf.

1998
The Baku region, and the Caspian Sea in general, becomes the focus of interest of oil companies.

1999
Petroleum is as inexpensive as bottled water and as cheap as it was before the energy crises of the 1970s.

2002
An oil workers' strike in Venezuela causes world oil prices to rise.

2003
Oil prices rise as a result of U.S.-led military intervention in Iraq.

Concept Web

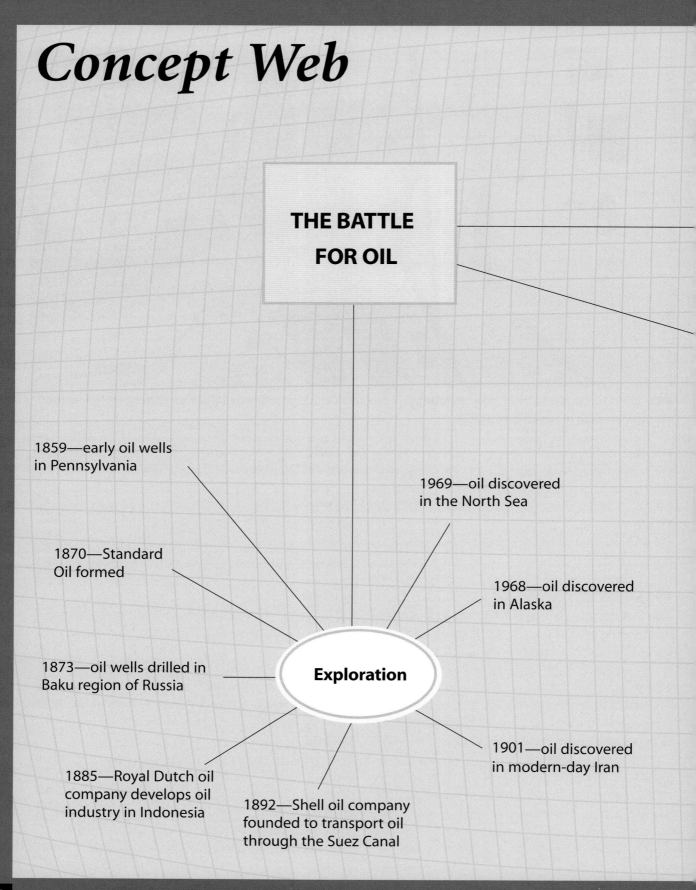

THE BATTLE
FOR OIL

Exploration

1859—early oil wells
in Pennsylvania

1870—Standard
Oil formed

1873—oil wells drilled in
Baku region of Russia

1885—Royal Dutch oil
company develops oil
industry in Indonesia

1892—Shell oil company
founded to transport oil
through the Suez Canal

1969—oil discovered
in the North Sea

1968—oil discovered
in Alaska

1901—oil discovered
in modern-day Iran

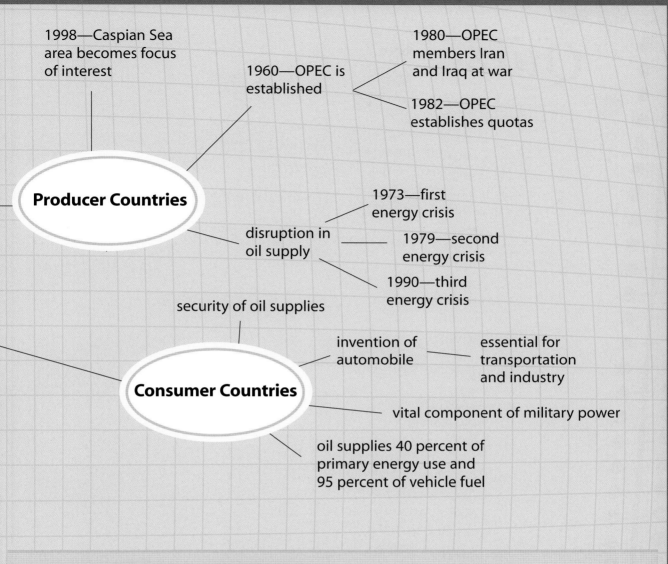

1998—Caspian Sea area becomes focus of interest

1960—OPEC is established

1980—OPEC members Iran and Iraq at war

1982—OPEC establishes quotas

Producer Countries

disruption in oil supply

1973—first energy crisis

1979—second energy crisis

1990—third energy crisis

security of oil supplies

Consumer Countries

invention of automobile

essential for transportation and industry

vital component of military power

oil supplies 40 percent of primary energy use and 95 percent of vehicle fuel

MAKE YOUR OWN CONCEPT WEB

A concept web is a useful summary tool. It can also be used to plan your research or help you write an essay or report. To make your own concept web, follow the steps below:

- You will need a large piece of unlined paper and a pencil.
- First, read through your source material, such as *The Battle for Oil* in the Understanding Global Issues series.
- Write the main idea, or concept, in large letters in the center of the page.
- On a sheet of lined paper, jot down all words, phrases, or lists that you know are connected with the concept. Try to do this from memory.
- Look at your list. Can you group your words and phrases in certain topics or themes? Connect the different topics with lines to the center, or to other "branches."
- Critique your concept web. Ask questions about the material on your concept web: Does it all make sense? Are all the links shown? Could there be other ways of looking at it? Is anything missing?
- What more do you need to find out? Develop questions for those areas you are still unsure about or where information is missing. Use these questions as a basis for further research.

Quiz

Multiple Choice

1. Which of the following statements about oil is false?
   a) Oil is one of the foundations of modern civilization.
   b) Oil is important to the plastics industry.
   c) Oil is a renewable resource.
   d) Oil is viewed as a cause of environmental degradation.

2. According to one prediction, how much oil will the United States need to import in 2025?
   a) 40 percent
   b) 50 percent
   c) 60 percent
   d) 70 percent

3. John D. Rockefeller founded which of these companies:
   a) Pemex
   b) Standard Oil
   c) Anglo-Persian
   d) Lukoil

4. Total world oil demand in 2003 was:
   a) 500,000 barrels a day
   b) 2 million barrels a day
   c) 53 million barrels a day
   d) 77 million barrels a day

5. What is the percentage of oil imported by the European Union?
   a) 20 percent
   b) 44 percent
   c) 65 percent
   d) 80 percent

6. How much oil is stored in the United States' Strategic Petroleum Reserve?
   a) 77 million barrels
   b) 100 million barrels
   c) 250 million barrels
   d) 600 million barrels

7. Wahhabism is:
   a) a new oil technology
   b) a type of sport utility vehicle
   c) a form of Islam
   d) an oil field in the Caspian Sea area

Where Did It Happen?

1. Oil wells were drilled here in 1859.
2. The largest proved reserves of oil are found here.
3. This country produced half the world's oil at the beginning of the twentieth century.
4. Al-Qaeda attacked a supertanker off the coast of this country.

True or False

1. The oil industry is immune to social concerns.
2. Oil is a vital component of military power.
3. Japan buys 80 percent of its oil from the Middle East.
4. OPEC was formed in 1970.

Answers on page 53

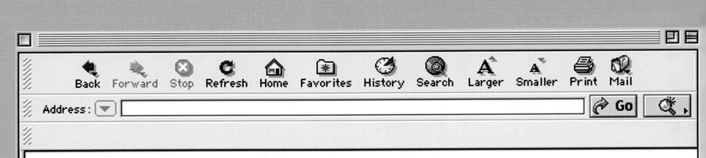

Internet Resources

The following websites provide more information about oil and the oil industry:

British Petroleum (BP)
www.bp.com/home.do
BP, once known as Anglo-Persian Oil Company, was founded in 1909. Every year since 1951, BP has published a report entitled the *BP Statistical Review of World Energy.* This report contains the latest facts about energy use around the world.

Energy Action
www.nef1.org/ea/home.html
The Energy Action website is dedicated to energy conservation, environmental stewardship, and the promotion of positive action through better energy education. This website contains a section for students, which includes activities and a literature section.

Energy Information Administration (EIA)
www.eia.doe.gov
The EIA contains the official energy statistics from the U.S. government. This website also contains an overview of the energy situation in countries around the world.

Some websites stay current longer than others. To find other websites related to oil and energy, enter terms such as "petroleum" and "oil" into a search engine.

Further Reading

Akiner, Shirin, and Anne Aldis, eds. *The Caspian: Politics, Energy and Security*. New York: RoutledgeCurzon, 2004.

Deffeyes, Kenneth S. *Hubbert's Peak: The Impending World Oil Shortage*. Princeton: Princeton University Press, 2003.

Heinberg, Richard. *The Party's Over: Oil, War and the Fate of Industrial Societies*. Gabriola, BC: New Society Publishers, 2003.

Klare, Michael T. *Resource Wars: The New Landscape of Global Conflict*. New York: Henry Holt, 2002.

Ratliff, William E. *Russian Oil in America's Future*. Stanford, CA: Hoover Institution on War, Revolution and Peace, Stanford University, 2003.

Answers

Multiple Choice
1. c)   2. d)   3. b)   4. d)   5. c)   6. d)   7. c)

Where Did It Happen?
1. Pennsylvania   2. Saudi Arabia   3. Russia   4. Yemen

True or False
1. F   2. T   3. T   4. F

Glossary

autocratic: characteristic of an absolute ruler or absolute rule; having absolute sovereignty

British thermal units: the amount of heat needed to raise the temperature of one pound of water by 1.0° Fahrenheit (0.6° Celsius)

cable-tool drilling: a method of drilling whereby an impact tool or bit, suspended in the well from a steel cable, is dropped repeatedly on the bottom of the hole to crush the rock

Caucasus: mountain range between the Black Sea and the Caspian Sea that forms part of the traditional border between Europe and Asia

concessions: contracts granting the right to operate a business

correlation: the degree to which two or more variables are related and change together

developed countries: countries that have strong economies and sophisticated industries; developed countries are also called industrialized countries

developing countries: countries that are undergoing the process of industrialization, sometimes collectively referred to as the "Third World"

industrialized: having developed industry

infrastructure: the systems that operate in a city, such as transportation, power, water, and sanitation systems

Islamist: an Islamic movement characterized by moral conservatism, literalism, and the attempt to implement Islamic values in all spheres of life

multinational: a large company with operations in more than one country

nationalism: the idea that one national culture and interests are superior to any other

paramilitaries: groups that are organized like an army but are not official and often not legal

pariah: a country, or person, that is avoided or not accepted by a social group because it is not respected or trusted

permafrost: ground that is permanently frozen

pharmaceuticals: involved in or associated with the manufacture, preparation, dispensing, or sale of medical drugs

philanthropists: people who make charitable donations intended to increase human well-being

privatization: transferring public property and services from public or government control to private control

quota: a prescribed number; a limit on exports or imports

recession: the state of the economy declines

reservoirs: natural or artificial places where liquid is collected

spare capacity: oil wells that can be put into production in a short period of time

Index

Credits

All of the Internet URLs given in the book were valid at the time of publication. However, due to the dynamic nature of the Internet, some addresses may have changed, or sites may have ceased to exist since publication. While the author and publisher regret any inconvenience this may cause readers, no responsibility for any such changes can be accepted by either the author or the publisher.

Every reasonable effort has been made to trace ownership and to obtain permission to reprint copyright material. The publishers would be pleased to have any errors or omissions brought to their attention so that they may be corrected in subsequent printings.